"ENLIGHTENED
IN THE
21ˢᵗ Century"

RICHARD KRAULAND

ISBN 978-1-64569-630-8 (paperback)
ISBN 978-1-64569-631-5 (digital)

Christian Faith Publishing, Inc.
832 Park Avenue
Meadville, PA 16335
www.christianfaithpublishing.com

Printed in the United States of America

Contents

Prologue

*Reality is that which, when you stop
believing in it, doesn't go away.*
— Philip K. Dick,
I Hope I Shall Arrive Soon

*Facts are stubborn things; and whatever
may be our wishes, our inclinations, or
the dictates of our passions, they cannot
alter the state of facts and evidence.*
— John Adams, second presi-
dent of the United States

The purpose of this book is to open people's minds, to help them tear down the walls that have separated them from God. These are walls they themselves have accepted as real. But they are not real. They believe there are contradictions between science and religion. In fact, there are not.

Science has given us many great things, like medical breakthroughs, rocket science, the internet, and all manner of things that are good and true. And they have given science a respected place in our culture. But what is science and what is not science? We need to separate real science from all the things that claim to be real science, but are not.

The real science certainly deserves our respect. But the nonreal science is actually the information, ideas, and theories that close our minds to the truth. We need to understand which of these ideas are out there and how they inject untrue concepts into our search for the truth.

By tearing through non-science's veil of credibility, we can open our minds to the truth of God's reality, and God's presence in our lives. By breaking through those barriers, the light of truth can shine through.

Introduction

OK, before we start, I'd like you to take a pencil or pen or crayon or a pointed stick, or whatever you can lay your hands on, and draw a picture, on the facing empty page here, of a tree. Any tree will do. Pick your favorite tree and just draw a picture of it. Don't worry about me. I'll wait here, and I'll hum the theme from the TV show *Jeopardy*, while I'm waiting for you. Please don't read on until you draw your tree.

Are you finished? Great. Unless you are a very rare individual, I'm willing to bet the tree you drew was actually only half of the tree. I would guess that over 99 percent of people will forget to draw the root system of the tree—that part of the tree, which we all know, is there. But because it is mostly out of sight, we simply forget about it. I call that shallow thinking. And we all do it, all the time. Obviously, no tree can exist without its root system. Its root system is a critical part of the entire living tree. But we just don't think about it.

This is a very simple example. But the fact is, we often forget things we know when we're making decisions or thinking about things, or more accurately, when we're not thinking about things. One of the themes we're going to explore in this book is just how much information there is, like that, which we know, but we usually don't think about. And we usually don't use it.

In the past 150 years or so, we (mankind) have researched nearly every area of curiosity. We can fly! We can see the inside of single cells and the tracks of exploding sub-atomic particles. We can see galaxies that are well over ten billion lightyears away. We have sent men to the moon and returned them safely. We have sent cameras and gathered images of every planet in our solar system and beyond. We have observed the fusion of atomic nuclei, split the atom, and manipulated DNA itself.

We have built robots that can do our work safely, and we have refined the collection, storage, and retrieval of data beyond our imaginations of just 25 years ago. These advances in learning are truly mind-boggling.

Mankind has learned a *lot* about almost everything. Although most normal people don't understand most of these advances, still we comfortably use medical, communication, transportation, entertainment, information, and other technologies every day. We trust the people who make these products. And we believe in the science that produced them. As we should. But are there limits to what we should accept as true?

The fact is that we, mankind, know a lot more than we, individually, think we know. The purpose of this book is to bring to the surface much of the information we know, but that we don't think about, or information that we individually don't know but that some researchers have discovered; so that we can now all know it. And also to expose a great deal of the information we think is true, but it's actually not true. In some cases, this is described as "common knowledge," which "everybody knows." The only problem with it is that some of it is not true. Once we get those things sorted out, we're going to find that we will make decisions, which are much better. And it will be much harder for anyone to successfully deceive us. I am talking about becoming *enlightened*. This is tremendously important for a successful life.

I am convinced that much of the problems in the world today are a result of people like us, and especially our leaders, making very bad decisions. They make these decisions poorly because they aren't using all the information that is available to them, or they are using information that is simply incorrect. And the real tragedy is that the incorrect information should be recognizable by all of us, but it isn't.

It is obvious to me that there is a universe of false information actively circulating in America today. Ideas that are widely believed to be true, but they are not true. These ideas permeate all walks of life: business, science, news, politics, economics, and even religion. Together, they form a body of work that opposes clear and honest thinking and good decision making. They stand in opposition to the truth. In many cases, these ideas support and reinforce each other. They serve to misinform and mislead people.

I occasionally wonder about what is feeding this misinformation. It seems to include poor, ineffective schools;

a failed media establishment; economic ignorance; and the growth of immorality; or at least, the absence of religious training.

The primary characteristic of being enlightened is that you can readily see that these false ideas are false. The truth becomes easily recognizable for enlightened people. The truth that is consistent with real observable scientific facts, economic realities, religious teachings, and your everyday real-life experiences.

I believe that being well-grounded in the truth is absolutely necessary for a successful life as a free person. So I intend to address many areas of human endeavors, in order to expose the misinformation, and reestablish the truth to its rightful place in our thinking. The good news is that the truth will be consistent with common sense and your day-to-day experiences, thereby making it readily recognizable. What it takes to "see" it is no more that looking a little deeper, in order to see the roots of the subject matter at hand.

Like your picture of the tree, once we think just a little more deeply, the true nature of the tree becomes quickly recognized, so it is with the truth. Get ready to learn. This is going to be great!

Once we get through this reading, I'm hoping that all of us will have a common understanding of what is true and what is real and what is not. If we can get to that type of shared wisdom, then we'll have a much better chance of having a successful and peaceful life together; sharing it with others and avoiding many of the unforced errors we all make every day.

That is another benefit of being enlightened. Knowing that which is known; that which is knowable but as yet unknown, and recognizing that some things can never be known, and being aware of the limitations that the missing knowledge imposes on us.

To get to that point, we need to develop a common understanding of truth, reality, science, and religion. And that's exactly what we are about to do. So let's get started.

Reality

What is reality? What is real?

I once heard someone say that the word *reality* should always be written with quotation marks around it. The idea is that each person has their own definition for reality. We define it based on our experiences and ideas, and there is no guarantee that our definition of reality is identical to anyone else's definition. In fact, since we all have a different set of experiences and ideas, it would be highly unlikely that two people would have an identical understanding of "reality," even if they grew up together.

So let's talk about what reality is. I think most people probably, at a minimum, define reality based upon what they can sense. What they can see, what they can hear, what they can feel, what they can taste, and what they can smell. Obviously, all those things are real.

Excluding cases of mental illness or delusions, certainly everything we can sense is real. You are hearing sounds right now. And all the things making those sounds are obviously real—similarly with the things we see. Those must also be real. We can see cars on roads. We can see furniture in the house. We can see buildings, the sky, the clouds, the ground, plants, and animals. Everything we see is unquestionably real, also with our sense of smell. Everything we can smell is certainly real. We can smell the food we're going to eat. We can smell the air around us. We can smell the flowers. We can smell the gasoline as we put it into our tanks. We can smell our houses. We can smell air fresheners. We can smell the fresh cut grass. Everything we smell is clearly real.

Likewise with what we can touch. Those things must also be real. Most of what we can see, we can also touch. So what we see, the reality of what we can see, is confirmed by the reality of what we can touch. And many times, most of the things that are real can be sensed with more than just one sense. We can touch and feel and smell and taste the same things; and in this way, we can confirm and further define what those things actually are.

However, we do have to make allowances for the fact that some people sense things that really are not there. These types of experiences may be caused by a brain injury, or by some type of physical or emotional traumatic event. In my own situation, I was once paralyzed from the neck down in a car accident. For a time, I could feel nothing. I could not move anything below my neck, and I was receiving no sensations of feeling whatsoever from my body.

In time, certain functions began to return, including the sense of feeling. Unfortunately, when the feeling came back to my left arm, what I began to feel was an extremely difficult burning sensation. This pain went down the upper side of my left forearm. In fact, to this day, I can still trace that line of pain, which has been burned into my memory.

At that time, I knew that my arm was not in a furnace. I knew that my arm was not on fire, but it felt as though it absolutely was. So when we talk about defining reality and using our senses to do it, we need to be a little bit careful to make sure we exclude these types of sensations, which can occur in situations where the person is not well physically, emotionally, or mentally.

Even in cases of perfect health, though, different people will sense things differently. As an old friend of mine use to say, "Some people don't like jelly donuts." And that's true. Our senses provide the raw data, but our individual brains process that data. And it is quite possible that two healthy people will sense things differently. One says it tastes good. The other says it tastes bad. One person in a room says it's too hot. The person next to them says it's too cold. But hey, whataya gonna do? The fact is that the room's temperature is 71 degrees Fahrenheit. Whether it is too hot or too cold is an opinion and subjective. It's important to separate the facts from the subjective opinions. We will be doing a lot of that as we move forward.

Two major questions present themselves now. If we are going to define so much of our "reality" by what we sense, then we better learn exactly how these senses work and what their limitations are. And secondly, what else is "real" besides what we can sense? Are there other things in the universe, other things in existence, that we will never be able to see or hear or feel or taste or smell or otherwise sense? In fact, we now know there are many. So let's look at some examples.

What we can see with our eyes, science has made quite clear to us, is actually a very narrow part of the electromagnetic spectrum. There are frequencies which are lower than our eyes can detect. These would be in the infrared range. Likewise, there are higher frequencies, which we cannot see. In this case, they are in the ultraviolet range.

What we see as different colors are actually the differences in the frequencies of the electromagnetic radiation within the visible range of the spectrum, which are hitting the retinas in our eyes. Our retinas contain structures referred to as cones. People who are born with too few cones are functionally colorblind because they cannot tell one color from another. These cones are what allow us to detect and distinguish the visible colors. Again, in reality, what we are actually detecting is different frequencies of electromagnetic vibrations, different frequencies of light.

What's actually out there in nature is not different colors. What's actually out there are different frequencies of electromagnetic radiation, which our minds are able to distinguish and perceive as colors. This color-detecting instinct helps us to distinguish things in our environment, which we need to understand and work with every day.

Another important point here is not only to understand what the nature of vision is and what the nature of colors are, but also that we are only seeing a small narrow cross-section of the electromagnetic spectrum. We do not for example see X-rays. They appear to be invisible to our eyes, yet we know they exist, and we have instrumentation to detect them. Likewise, radio stations and television stations are constantly broadcasting electromagnetic radiation, which is traveling through our cities and towns, traveling in every direction through the air, our homes, and even our bodies. And we can't see them because those frequencies are beyond the range of what our eyes can detect. So obviously, there is much more in reality than our eyes can detect.

The same is true with our hearing. While we can hear many sounds, there are many more we cannot hear. What we perceive as sounds are actually waves of air pressure, which vary in frequency and amplitude. The way that sound works is that the air around us contains countless changes in air pressure waves. When these waves reach our inner ears, those oscillations create sympathetic vibrations in very small hairs that exist in our cochleae. As those small hairs vibrate they excite nerves, which send electrochemical signal into our brains. The signals are then picked up by our brains and are perceived as sounds. I still don't understand how that perception process works, even though I'm doing it every waking moment.

But your "hearing" process is just beginning. After the sounds are perceived, another part of your brain has to recognize what you are hearing. Is it a car horn? Or a dog barking? Or a human voice? Or something else? And if it is a human voice, then what language is being spoken? And once the language is recognized, what words are you hearing? And what do those words mean? Each one of these questions indicates a discrete mental process, which must occur in sequence. And together, these processes get conflated into one function known as "hearing." Obviously, hearing is a very complex process, which includes many other parts of the brain, and not just our ears.

So even though everything we hear is real, clearly there are many things we do not hear that are also real. Probably the most common example of this, which people may have an experience with, is a dog whistle. If someone is standing next to you, and they blow into a dog whistle, you will not hear a sound. However, if you happen to have a dog nearby that dog will respond to it because dogs have cochleae, which can pick up frequencies that ours cannot. So it's clear that there are many other subsonic and ultrasonic frequencies, which you simply cannot pick up. The fact that we cannot hear them does not mean they are not there. They are in fact there, and we know that because we've created tools, which allow us to detect things that our senses cannot.

Before we leave the subject of our hearing, a fascinating story was being widely publicized while I was writing this. The story was presented as "yanny" (rhymes with uncanny) or "laurel." A sound was recorded and played back. Some people clearly hear the word *laurel.*, while people right next to them clearly heard the word *yanny*. Obviously, these two words sound nothing alike. So what was going on?

In fact, in my case, it got even weirder. I first saw the story early one morning on the national news. I clearly heard *laurel*. Because I am interested in this kind of news story, I recorded it to show my wife. Later that day, I replayed my recording. This time, I could only hear *yanny*. The next morning, I played it back again, and then I could only hear *laurel.* Later that second morning, I could only hear *yanny* again. So what the heck was going on?

Fortunately, on the third day, one cable network presented a guest specialist on the subject of hearing. He showed a graph of the sound that was being played and explained that people whose brain focused on the higher frequencies of the sound heard *laurel.* While those, whose brains focused on the low points in the frequencies, heard the word *yanny.* Apparently, my brain tended to focus on the higher frequencies in the mornings and on the lower frequencies later in the day.

But the fascinating point is that two people can receive identical sonic inputs and hear completely different sounds, due to the way their brains processed the electrochemical signals coming from their ears. This could be a real challenge to our efforts to develop a consensus on the nature of reality. But it is extremely important for us to face the fact that such things are possible, strange as that may seem.

So we need to open our minds to a much greater reality than what we can actually hear, see, taste, touch, and smell. I believe *that* much should be obvious to everyone. The unanswered question of course is what else is out there. How much is out there that we cannot sense? That's the big question—just how vast is reality and how much of it do we need to understand to know what's right and true, and what is not?

Let's look at the example of the Hubble space telescope. With the Hubble telescope positioned above our atmosphere, we have been able to see other galaxies, other stars, nebulas, and other structures in the universe, which are literally billions of lightyears away from earth. Because of the use of that instrument, we are now aware that the universe is incredibly large. In fact, everywhere we look in every direction, we see more galaxies. These are scientifically observable facts. You know, it's interesting that at one time in man's history, when we had no tools to help us, we would wake up in the morning and see the sunrise, watch it move across the sky and see it set, and people concluded then that we were standing still and the sun was moving around us. Actually that's a pretty straightforward observation.

As time went on, however, astronomers learned how to take very specific measurements of just how things moved across the sky. With the work of Copernicus, Galileo, and others, we eventually came to see that the sun was not moving around our fixed position. In truth, we are on a planet that is rotating and that rotation is what causes the sun to appear to be moving across our sky. So when we wake up in the morning now, and we see the sunrise or the sunset, we are still seeing the exact same things that our early ancestors saw. But we understand it differently. Our world has not changed. The sun is still moving across the sky. And it changes position with each season. And it repeats its positions each year. However, what has changed is our understanding of what is going on. Although our scientific observations are identical today to what they were thousands of years ago, our understanding has changed because we now have a greater awareness of what we're looking at. We have a better perspective today. And that new perspective makes us better informed. This type of increased awareness has resulted in major changes in our understanding of reality. In fact, it virtually every field of study, we have added to our level of awareness.

Here's a similar example from the field of microbiology. Dr. Louis Pasteur produced his rudimentary microscopes. And by doing so, he was able to peer down and see very small things. He was able to see bacteria and other disease-causing agents. He discovered an entirely new realm, which people never knew existed. Actual organisms living in their own ecosystem, too small to been seen by people with their naked eyes. Amazing. Before and after Dr. Pasteur's work, these bacteria continued to work as they always have. They cause food to waste away. They cause plant life to decay. They cause sickness in people and animals. People saw these signs, but didn't really understand what was going on. No doubt people thought they did know. They had their theories, like "evil spirits," or whatever. The fact is, every one of those earlier theories has since been proven to be incorrect.

Pick any field of study and the same story repeats itself. Planetary science is another example. Before we sent the Voyager spacecraft, the Cassini spacecraft, and the European spacecrafts, we had a very rudimentary knowledge of our solar system. However, now that we've actually landed crafts on other planets, on other moons, even on an asteroid, we know a great deal more about these heavenly bodies. And although they're doing the same thing they've always done, our older theories about them have been proven to be completely wrong. What's changed dramatically is our increased awareness of their nature, their properties, and their behavior. Thanks to science.

I think it's an interesting fact that every scientific theory that mankind has ever had has been proven to be false, except for the theories that we currently hold to be true. And I have little doubt, although I can't prove it that many of the theories we currently hold will likewise be proven false. Our continuing growth in scientific knowledge and our increasing awareness of the universe will provide more data, which will disprove our current theories and lead to the next generation of better theories. Actually, that's how science has always worked. Right?

Before we leave the subject of astronomy, I'd like to talk about how big our reality is. We need to point out that, just as the universe gets bigger and bigger and bigger, the farther we are able to look outward. The truth is that the universe also gets bigger and bigger and bigger as we look at smaller and smaller spaces. We have built superconducting supercolliders that are able to display and observe subatomic particles. As their pieces scatter, we are able to detect those smaller particles. The more energy we put into the collisions, the more particles we see. So while we once thought the atom was the smallest particle in existence, we now know the atom is made up of electrons and protons and neutrons. And we know that each of those particles is likewise made up of smaller particles—quarks muons, leptons, and so on, which at this point at least, appear to be the smallest particles known to man. That does *not* mean, however, that they are the smallest particles in existence. Science seems to tell us, over and over again, that there is always something new over the horizon. We just need to find a way to look there.

In fact, if you think about it, there cannot possibly be a "smallest particle." If there was, imagine that you could see it. There it is—the smallest possible thing. Right there in your mind's eye. But wait a minute. If it's a "thing," then it must be made of something. Is it hard or soft? If you cut it in half, what's inside? What color is it? And if you just cut in into two smaller pieces, then I guess, it wasn't the smallest thing after all. Was it? And if it was too hard to cut in half, then what makes it so hard? It must be made out of something.

The truth is that this question of the "smallest thing" has been discussed for millennia. Scientists actually thought they had it figured out for a while. When the "standard model of the atom" was developed and the periodic table began to be filled out with the discovery of more and more elements, it seemed that mankind had discovered the smallest things. Atoms. Atoms behaved differently depending on the number of protons, neutrons, and electrons each atom had. The science of chemistry was born, and it could accurately explain and predict how different elements behaved. And chemists understood why they behaved as they did. Chemistry really does explain just about everything we can see, hear, smell, taste, and touch.

This really was an astounding success for real science—a triumph of the scientific method of observation, hypothesis, experimentation, and observation. And if we had stopped right there, we could have felt pretty comfortable about our scientific knowledge.

Unfortunately (just kidding), you know how scientists are. Some of them wanted to know more about what these electrons, neutrons, and protons were made of. Instead of just declaring victory at the discoveries made in the field of chemistry, scientist moved on to the study of, what has become known as, particle physics. And their superconducting, supercollider in Switzerland has expanded their vision into another even smaller realm.

As we go into the realms of the smaller and smaller and smaller, infinity seems to extend itself, just as the universe seems to extend itself as we get into the realm of the bigger and bigger and bigger. In fact, it seems to me that science has already shown us that the universe is infinitely small, just as it is infinitely big. The further our scientific instruments allow us to see, the more there is to see.

But if we think about this, an amazing reality comes into view. Let's think about something as simple as an oxygen molecule, which is made up of two oxygen atoms. This oxygen molecule is very important to all living things. In fact, the energy I am using right now to write this book is a result of biochemical processes, which involves oxygen molecules. Clearly there are countless trillions of oxygen molecules floating around the earth and elsewhere. The amazing thing to me is that the same oxygen molecules that are in my body right now are working in identical fashion to all the oxygen molecules that are in your body right now, as you are reading this book. Likewise, no doubt there are people in China and South America and Africa and everywhere who are breathing in other oxygen molecules. In all of us, countless trillions of oxygen molecules are the exact same size, and they all are working exactly the same way. In fact, the billions of oxygen molecules I breathed in an hour ago are working exactly the same as the billion I am breathing in right now. And the molecules that are feeding your life's energy are all working the same as every other oxygen molecule in the universe.

We now know there is oxygen in the form of water on Mars, and on the moon, and in other places in the solar system. Isn't it incredible that every oxygen molecule is the same size as all the rest, and they all behave exactly the same as all the rest of them. In fact, the science of chemistry explains how you can breathe in any one of these oxygen molecules, and it will perform for you, flawlessly, in the same fashion as every other oxygen molecule.

That is an incredible realization. Can you think of the countless trillions of oxygen molecules throughout the universe, and all of them, at least all that we've ever encountered—all behave exactly the same. And it's not just oxygen. Every element on the periodic table displays this same characteristic of universally uniform behavior. And when you think about it, each one of these individual molecules is made up of an infinitely small universe, which contains electrons, protons, neutrons, and every other type of infinitesimal subatomic particles—all behaving in a perfectly consistent way.

Given the fact that everything we know is made up of matter and energy, and that all matter and energy behave perfectly consistently at all times and all places, it's actually truthful to say that we live in a perfect world. A perfect universe in the sense that every single particle, every single piece of matter, every single quantum of energy, performs consistently as every other particle of the same type. We *know* this. Real science has learned it is true.

The big questions really are why? What exactly is holding it all together? What, or who, has created and is enforcing these laws of physics?

Let's keep going...

Science

Isn't science great? Let's just take minute to list some of the benefits to mankind that have come from the study of science:

Clean water
X-rays and MRIs
Antibiotics
Vaccines
Video games
Virtual reality
Heart, knee, and hip, transplants
Trains, planes, and automobiles
Roads and expressways
Men on the moon
Worldwide instantaneous communications
Television and radio
Supercomputers
The internet
Handheld GPS systems
Credit cards
ATMs

Atomic power plants
Safe drilling and mining equipment
Much more productive farming
Refrigeration
Fruits and vegetables all year around

Well, you get the idea. Clearly, science is real. And all of us have benefitted greatly from scientific discoveries and the study of science. But do we ever stop to ask, just what is "science?"

I think a good way to answer that question is to understand something called the scientific method.

The scientific method requires that in order to establish that a hypothesis is actually a scientific fact; experimental conditions have to be recreated, reproduced, in multiple experiments, all the while obtaining the same outcomes. This is how real science works—observations, followed by new hypotheses, followed by experimentation, then more observations. This cycle repeated endlessly is how we continue to reliably learn about our universe. And once those hypotheses are turned into scientific facts, they can be relied upon to support new ideas that will solve our problems and make our lives better. Science is a significant part of our search for truth. Much more to come on the subject of truth.

Everyone should believe in science.

OK, if that is what science is, then what is not science? What is fake science? Unfortunately, there is a lot of fake science going around these days. I'm going to talk about three of the most contentious issues in today's religious and political environment. And fake science is at the center of all three. They are

1. Evolution
2. Climate change, and
3. The big bang

Evolution

Let's start with evolution. Many books have been written that set up evolution as an alternative to the creationism of the Bible. School boards and their communities have been torn apart arguing which of these concepts should be taught in schools. But do they even empirically contradict each other?

To my way of thinking, evolution does successfully describe the way that life, in all its forms, is altered by its environment. Through the process of natural selection, those representatives of any species, which exhibit features that are best adapted to their current environment, are most likely to succeed, to survive. Those individuals who are poorly adapted to their current conditions are less likely to survive. And since the environment is constantly changing in natural, bounded, cyclical, ways, then it is no wonder that those who cannot survive the extremes are no longer with us.

A good example of this would be these new "super-bugs." These are the strains of bacteria that have become resistant to almost all antibiotics. Over decades of successful development of various antibacterial drugs, medicine has unwittingly cleared the field for those few germs, which are capable of surviving those drugs. Without competitors, these strains are free to multiply with impunity. And today, they represent a significant threat to human life.

Furthermore, in current times, there are readily available opportunities for scientist to make observations, which clearly support their theories concerning the effect of environment on the evolution of species. The island continent of Australia, with its unique marsupial populations, provides many such examples. It's hard to argue with valid observations. After all, facts are facts.

So what's the problem? Well, in their zeal to "discover" new things, some evolutionary scientists have made an intellectually fatal mistake. They have theorized about the *origin* of life on earth and the nature of past evolution and what it must have looked like, in order to get us to where we are today. Thus they created their assertions that current humans were descended from apes. In fact, they have even attempted to project back much, much, further.

Virtually every school in the country has textbooks, which illustrate a timeline where fish evolve into amphibians and amphibians into land animals, which eventually get to monkeys, and then to humans. But is this science? Is this a scientific fact? Clearly it is not. At least not yet. Because no scientist has ever witnessed the origin of a newly living cell, or one simpler species changing into another more complex one. And until we invent a time machine to go back to make the necessary observations, evolution will forever be just a theory. No more, no less. Scientifically, it can explain some changes in living organisms, but it does not apply to the origins of life.

So why has every child in America been taught that it is a scientific fact? At this point, their teachers were probably taught the same thing. Perhaps their parents were too? So they just accept it implicitly. And once again, a fake science idea has crept its way into the study of science. This is very problematical. Because science is a search for truth. And nontruth needs to be weeded out. Not added in. In closing, I am *not* claiming the evolution has been disproven as a possible source of life in the universe. I am only saying that this theory can never be proven or disproven by our accepted scientific methods. It's too late to make those observations. And neither conclusion should be taught as having a firm basis in fact. At least, not yet.

Creationism

Now, regarding creationism. In Western culture, this explanation for the origin of life is believed to have been provided to mankind through the divine revelations provided to us in the Hebrew Bible. Again, like evolution, it's way too late to prove or disprove these assertions by using our scientific methods. You either believe them or you don't. But before you decide, how about looking into the realm of real science to see if there is any direct evidence one way or the other?

Since the subject at hand is the origin of life, it might be helpful to look toward what we know about the nature of life. In recent years, real science has done a magnificent job of mapping the genome of a few species, including the human genome. This is a monstrous achievement, which has the potential to hugely benefit, or hugely damage, the future of humanity.

[Aside: Like the discovery of atomic power, this achievement reminds me that mankind's technological achievements must never get too far ahead of our moral and ethical development. Truly catastrophic consequences are possible if we proceed without the proper moral guidance. And a crucial question is, where will that guidance come from? I am hoping to contribute to that guidance through this work.]

So what do we know about DNA and how it works? When a human egg is fertilized, half of its chromosomes come from each parent. It literally begins with one cell, which quickly becomes two, then four, then eight, sixteen, thirty-two, and so on, eventually topping out in excess of 37,000,000,000,000 cells. During its development, which is guided by its DNA structure, the embryo begins to differentiate into a variety of different types of cells—skin cells, bone cells, liver cells, kidney cells, blood cells, nerve cells, brain cells, stomach cells, intestinal cells, and so on.

Real science has convincingly determined that each cell contains the entire DNA package of this new human being. That is, the original set of chromosomes is reproduced and passed on to every one of the 37,000,000,000,000 plus cells to come. And that DNA set contains the instructions on how to make each one of those different types of cells. That is amazing. But not as amazing as what comes next.

Knowing how to make a lot of different cells is a magnificent achievement for a DNA molecule and replicating and passing a duplicate copy of yourself on to every cell is also pretty spectacular. But there's another achievement of DNA that most people don't think about. That is the timing mechanism.

It would not do much good if the embryo had bone cells growing in their brain area or heart area. Or to have liver or kidney cells where your skin is supposed to be. Or skin cells where your eyes are supposed to be, or eyes where your blood is supposed to be. Somehow, in addition to growing differentiated cells, DNA also knows when and where to grow each type of cell! And the placements of these cells are there to solve problems that won't be encountered until the fetus is born, grown, and trying to survive in the outside world, an environment that the DNA has never experienced.

In fact, if the term *intelligent design* doesn't apply to the structure of DNA, then I don't know what does. All the observations the evolutionary real scientists make, presume the preexistence, and functioning of DNA. And the natural selection processes that alter DNA from generation to generation are coming from external factors in the environment.

I am arguing here that it stands to reason that no evolutionary process could simultaneously develop the following three things: (1) the "programming" necessary to create the correct wide variety of all necessary cell types; (2) the timing mechanism to create and place each of the trillions of cells in its proper location; and (3) the mechanism to recreate the DNA itself to pass along those developments to all those other cells. Any random evolutionary trial-and-error process would fail a countless number of times. And each failure would result in the death of that evolutionary process, requiring everything to begin to re-evolve again.

The only idea that makes any sense is that these three capabilities were created simultaneously, by an intellect that understood the demands that the external environment would eventually place on this life form. And the fact that this programming occurred at the molecular level, to solve those real-life problems at our daily level, again implies that an overarching consciousness was involved. Further supporting this argument is the concurrent development of vegetable life forms. Plants convert carbon dioxide into breathable oxygen. Animals convert oxygen into carbon dioxide. Neither form could survive for long without the others' presence. This again argues for the contemporary creation of both. Perhaps within six days?

And one more piece of supportive evidence from the real molecular scientists—the structure of DNA is at least somewhat understood. It primarily consists of four component molecules usually abbreviated as C, A, T, and G. C and G are usually paired in the double-helix structure, as are A and T. Those who are familiar with basic machine languages might see this as a possible base-four programming language. Although we may not yet know how to engineer this programming, one thing is very clear—DNA *is* an engineerable structure.

So my conclusion on this question about the origin of life is that no person will ever know, for a scientific fact, exactly how life began on earth. At this point, it is a matter of faith, no matter which explanation you choose to believe. In fact, the correct explanation may be something completely different from the options we are considering today.

But we do know some things from our study of real science. And those (recently developed) facts about DNA make it very clear that some random evolutionary process could not have been the source of life on our planet. It just doesn't stand to reason, given all that we know about the workings of DNA. The real science clearly supports some theory involving intelligent design by an overarching consciousness. Nevertheless, our schools continue to misinform their students. That will make it more difficult for those students to develop a proper, truthful, and integrated understanding of the universe. And it also makes it more difficult for our society at large to join in a common understanding about what is true and what is not. That is the ultimate cost of fake science. And it is tragically significant.

Climate Change

So let's move on to another extremely divisive subject in modern society. Climate change was originally known as global warming. But as the real science measurements failed to show the expected rise in global temperatures, the name was changed. But the ferocity of its adherents has not diminished. No doubt, when you believe the future of mankind is at stake, it is right and proper to do everything you can do to save the planet. That is totally right and proper.

In the past few decades, many billions of dollars have been invested in the study of our atmosphere, with an emphasis on evaluating the effects of manmade climate change. Given the magnitude of the issue, it's readily understandable that the United Nations would get in involved. It's Intergovernmental Panel on Climate Change (IPCC) has issued massive analyses. And well-attended international conferences in Kyoto, Copenhagen, and elsewhere have issued major warnings and quantified goals for reducing carbon dioxide (CO_2) emissions. True believers now claim that the science is "settled" and that there is an international consensus that manmade, damaging, climate change is a scientific fact. Of course, such an important subject has become a major political issue in the United States, as the two major political parties have pretty much come down on opposite sides of the issue.

Those who do not accept the "settled science" of climate change are being called *science deniers*. And even their morality is being called into question. So, is this settled science fact, or not?

Once again, I seek guidance from the real science world. It has been credibly demonstrated as a scientific fact that CO_2 is indeed a greenhouse gas. It has unique heat retention characteristics, which help to keep the earth warm during the night time, as does water vapor and the other gases in the atmosphere, according to their own properties. And as we add CO_2 to the atmosphere, we are most likely having some effect on global temperatures.

The big question of course is, how much of an effect does it have? That's a tough question to answer. Today CO_2 represents only about 0.0004 of the gasses in our air. That's four parts per ten thousand. There is actually much, much more argon in the earth's atmosphere than there is CO_2. Even if the level of CO_2 we're to someday increase to five parts per ten thousand would that really have any noticeable effect? It seems unlikely to me, but I admit that I do not know. At this point, we also need to appreciate the fact that the earth's climate is an incredibly complex system, with amazing corrective processes to keep things in equilibrium. As such, we do not yet fully understand all those processes.

Virtually all of the alarm about climate change is driven by predictions of future temperature increases. Such increases are expected to cause a rise in sea level, with disastrous consequences for coastal population centers, and an increase in the frequency of extreme weather events. All these predictions are based on very complex computer models, which attempt to simulate the actual atmosphere of the earth. Fortunately, I do know something about computer models.

To get a valid climate prediction, we need three things—first, supercomputers that are fast enough to run the complex climate models. Those we have. Advances in computer processing speed have achieved incredible results. Supercomputers can perform many trillions of calculations per minute. So the necessary hardware is in place to run these models.

Secondly, we need a model that is complex enough to correctly simulate the atmosphere of the earth. We do not yet have that. When you consider that virtually everything affects the atmosphere, even external factors like the surface of the sun—it's hard for me to imagine that we will ever have a thorough enough understanding of all the relevant factors, to ever create a reliable model. But that's just my opinion. And I'm willing to keep an open mind on that subject. No doubt, real science has achieved incredible advances no one could've imagined many years earlier. So it is possible we may have a reliable model at some point in the future. But not today.

And thirdly, we need a data set at t=0 to initiate the model. This would necessarily include numbers for: temperature, wind speed, wind direction, relative humidity, barometric pressure, ground temperature, ocean temperature, ocean currents, cloud opacity, sunlight, solar winds, precipitation, etc., for every place and every altitude on earth, simultaneously. We don't have those. In fact, we never will. We will always have to use proxies or estimates to fill in the data's blanks.

And then there is the error factor. For example, if someone were to ask you what the high temperature was for your city, the day before yesterday, you could go to an authoritative source and look that up. Let's say you learned that the high was 72 degrees Fahrenheit. That's a historical fact. No problem. Right? Well, hold on a minute. If the actual high were 72.4 degrees, it would still have been reported as 72. Likewise, if the actual high was 71.8, it would have been reported as 72. In fact, the number 72 actually represents the range from 71.5 to 72.5 degrees. Now, let's say you also learned that yesterday's high temperature was 75 degrees. Again, that 75 really represents the range from 74.5 to 75.5.

Now, if you were then asked to calculate the total of yesterday's high temperature, plus the previous day's high, you would reasonably and honestly answer that the total was 147—72 plus 75. However, in reality, the total could have been as low as 146, or as high as 148. There is a significant error factor created by simply adding two recent historical numbers together. Every single mathematical calculation actually serves to compound the error factor in the final answer.

So it should be obvious now that the trillions of calculations, which occur as our complex climate model runs, would serve to compound the error factor to an astronomical level, thereby making the outputs completely useless. That's worth repeating. Every complex computer model, climate or otherwise, will always have an error factor that overwhelms its actual outputs. The best examples of such models are the complex econometric models, which have been running for decades, attempting to make accurate financial projections. They simply don't work. That's a historical fact too.

So any climate predictions that are based on computer climate models simply aren't worth the paper they are printed on. That's not my opinion. That's a scientific fact based on the nature of numbers and the error factors, which are a part of the very nature of numbers.

So...is there *anything* in the real science world that might give us some idea about the future of the earth's climate? Yes, fortunately there is. About 20 years ago, I saw a graph of the Earth's temperatures over the past 400,000 years. It caught my attention because it showed that something had changed dramatically about 10,000 years ago.

You can find the same information if you go to your favorite search engine and lookup "history of earth temperatures". There is a link out there to "Earth Temperatures: a Brief History of Recent Changes...". As you will see, the very first chart shows a graph of the history of the earth's temperatures over the past four hundred thousand years.

To be honest, I cannot assess how accurate these measurements are. But to my knowledge, they represent the best measurements we have, and they are not being actively disputed.

As you can see, for the first 390,000 years, this graph represents a classic pattern common to natural, chaotic, bounded systems. It demonstrates long cycles, short cycles, and everything in between. The big surprise occurs in the last 10,000 years. Here the temperatures break from their historic pattern and begin to converge on a set temperature. Three interesting facts are evident: first, over these past 10,000 years, the variations in temperatures are actually decreasing, as the temperatures converge to the new average. Secondly, this new average temperature is significantly higher than the average that existed for the previous 390,000 years. And thirdly, this new temperature, which we experience every day, just happens to be very beneficial for human habitation and agriculture.

It looks as if *something* has altered and stabilized the earth's climate into a range that is very beneficial for life on earth, as we know it, dominated by mankind. That's just an observation based on the available data. The fact is that mankind has spread across the globe and is thriving under our current conditions. And these conditions had not existed prior to ten thousand years ago. *Something*, or *someone*, has altered the earth's climate in a way that benefits mankind. And it happened about ten thousand years ago. Those are real scientific facts.

I have no idea what could change the climate pattern so dramatically. It seems like it would have to involve a change in the earth's orbit, or some other astronomical alterations, that would have planet-wide effects. But that's a guess. The fact remains that the change occurred, and it has proven to be tremendously beneficial for us all.

My conclusion is that we should all relax. Count our blessings. And stop worrying about what flawed predictions are telling us. There is a greater power at work here, which has taken great care of us. If you believe that power is conscious or not, it is still working on our behalf. I, of course, believe that everything happens for a reason.

The Big Bang

No doubt that the big bang theory is one of the greatest theories in the history of human science, if for no other reason that it is making a good faith effort to answer maybe the greatest question of all time. Using science to do so. That is, where did *everything* come from?

Basically, the theory holds the entire universe burst into existence about 13.5 billion years ago, from a single point. Initially it was infinitely hot, so hot that matter could not exist. As time went on, and this energy spread out, it began to cool off. The cooling process eventually allowed sub-atomic particles to solidify, then atoms, hydrogen atoms, the simplest of all atoms.

As time went on, according to the theory, the hydrogen atoms were attracted to each other in huge clouds. The clouds eventually became so dense they collapsed under their own gravity to form the first stars. In those stars, nuclear fusion converted the hydrogen into all the other elements on the periodic table, beginning with helium. Eventually *everything* material in the entire universe was formed through generation after generation of fusion—all occurring inside stars.

And all this occurred in about 13,500,000,000 years. Actually, that's pretty quick work. Currently, scientists, real scientists, believe there are over 2,000,000,000,000 galaxies in the visible universe, each containing approximately 100,000,000,000 stars, probably more. And using our own star as a typical solar system, which is estimated to contain about 1.2 times 10 to the 56th power atoms. Multiplying that times 100 billion stars and 2 trillion galaxies implies that the currently visible universe consists of 24,000,000, 000,000,000,000,000,000,000,000,000,000,000,000,000 ,000,000,000,000,000,000,000,000,000,000,000 atoms. Dividing by those 13.5 billion years mean that, on average, the universe has formed 1,770,000,000,000,000,000,000, 000,000,000,000,000,000,000,000,000,000,000,000 ,000,000,000 atoms per year, all by itself. Like I said, that's pretty quick work. And that's only the *visible* universe. And all this was supposed to have happened by pure random chance.

I'm sorry, but I just can't believe this, for the following reasons:

1. There is absolutely *nothing* in my experience, your experience, or the experience of any real scientist that could explain even one atom popping up out of nothing, yet alone the entire universe. In

fact, one of the laws of physics, the "conservation of matter and energy," specifically prohibits such spontaneous creation.

2. This big bang theory (BBT) makes no effort to explain the origins of the laws of physics, which it relies on to explain the evolution of the universe. Where did those laws come from? And how are those laws being consistently enforced across the entire universe for billions of years?

3. The big bang is clearly not a scientific fact because it was not observed and cannot be recreated using our scientific method.

4. The Hubble telescope and other telescopes are being used by real scientists to explore the most distant visible reaches of our universe. Their observations are *not* consistent with the BBT. As a result, new theoretical ideas about dark matter and dark energy have been developed to reconcile the real scientific data with the fake science of the BBT. And,

5. The real science of atomic fusion has no explanation for how any element heavier than iron could have been formed in the interior of stars. And well over one hundred other heavier elements are known to mankind.

Despite all these weaknesses in the BBT, I cannot turn on a single relevant program on the Science Channel, or on a PBS station, or even on NASA TV, that doesn't present the BBT as a scientific fact. It is not. Once again, we have an example of fake science being repeatedly, falsely, presented to the public as real science. Again, real science is a search for truth. Fake science only pollutes and conceals the search for truth, thereby making the truth more difficult to find.

I cannot explain why well-intentioned scientists have fallen into this sad diversion from real science. But I can say one thing for certain. That is, if the big bang theory is supposed to replace the idea of the creator's role in the beginning of the universe; then it has failed. Even though this fallacious theory is being repeated over and over, ad nauseam, it simply does not hold up to our real scientific standards. It is not consistent with actual scientific observations.

You and I need to face one very important fact. Science, real science, does not have a credible explanation for the beginning of the universe. It just doesn't. The BBT is no more provable than the creation story related in the Hebrew Bible. You can choose to believe in whatever you want. It's a free country. But please don't believe that your choice is a proven scientific fact. In reality, your choice is an act of faith. And if you are choosing to believe in the BBT, then you are ignoring actual scientific observations.

As we proceed through this discussion, we are going to continue to test these assumptions about science. We're going to see that we don't know as much as we think we know. We're going to clear away a lot of the fog that fake science is putting out. And hopefully, we will catch a glimpse of the truth based on real science, logic, and our own life experiences.

I ask only that you keep an open mind. Keep thinking for yourself. And don't be afraid of experiencing the real truth. Change is difficult. And it's not easy to realize that much of what you know may not be true. But the truth is well worth the effort needed to know it. In fact, I am hereby requesting that if I am presenting anything here that you know is not true, please contact me to straighten me out. I would be eternally grateful to anyone who would teach me something that is truthful.

The Human Body

Each of us cares greatly about our own good health, the health of our family and friends, and hopefully, the health of others as well. But how many of us have ever really thought deeply about everything our health depends on. Putting it another way: what all has to be right for any person to be healthy? Let's look.

First of all, as a single person, we need to avoid things like getting run over by a truck, falling off a cliff, getting blown apart by an explosion, and things like that. Most people are pretty good at avoiding those kinds of external threats to our bodies. And certainly, everyone who is healthy right now has managed to avoid such calamities.

But what about inside our skin? Our bodies consist of a collection of different systems—the cardiovascular system, the skeletal system, the nervous system, the digestive system, the autoimmune system, and so on. To be healthy, all these systems must be working well. And there are diseases, which attack these systems. Our study of medicine has made great progress in treating adverse developments in many of these systems. But what are these systems made out of?

Our internal systems consist primarily of organs. The nervous system includes the brain, spinal column, and all the nerves that run throughout our bodies. The digestive system includes our mouth, esophagus, stomach, small and large intestines, and so on. All our organs—heart, liver, kidneys, various glands, epidermis, lungs, etc., are all a part of one or another of these systems. And every organ must be functioning well to be a healthy person. Organs can be damaged by many things, including trauma, old age, infection, or other forms of deterioration. And each organ must be working in perfect concert with all the other organs in order to successfully coexist inside the very confined space of a singly human body. I think it is amazing that so many different organs can operate in such perfect harmony with each of the others. But what are our organs made out of?

Each of our organs is made up of cells—very specific, highly differentiated cells. Within each organ, these cells work as a team to perform the functions that the organ is responsible for. Liver cells, brain cells, bone cells, muscle cells, kidney cells, blood cells, heart cells, lung cells, and all the others need to be in the right place, doing the right things at all times for a body to be healthy. And cells can be attacked by infections, viruses, bacteria, or even a body's own immune system. Every cell is a separate living organism that is dependent on all its neighboring cells to live, function, and reproduce. But what are cells made up of?

Cells are made up of protein chains, which determine the purpose and structures within each cell. When looking into the functions within a single cell we enter into the realm of biochemistry. Proteins are made up of highly complex molecules. Those molecules are constructed inside the cells by the DNA and RNA that exists in every cell's nucleus. The molecules are made up of complex combinations of atoms. Atoms are the subject of the science of chemistry. Atoms consist of subatomic particles, which are studied in the field of particle physics.

What's interesting in all this is that subatomic particles are not aware of atoms. Atoms aren't aware of molecules. Molecules aren't aware of proteins. Proteins aren't aware of cells. Cells aren't aware of organs. Organs aren't aware of systems. Systems aren't aware of what is going on outside our bodies. And we aren't usually aware of any of this, unless we are suffering from a particular illness. Despite the ubiquitous lack of awareness, each one of these levels depends upon, and is driven by the level just below it. Life itself, like everything else, exists because of the nature of subatomic particles. And something, or someone, has organized all these particles, atoms, molecules, proteins, cells, organs, and systems, so we can survive and multiply on this earth for the many years of our lives.

The foresight, consciousness, and organizational skills that are needed to do that are so far beyond our comprehension that we can barely imagine that such skills even exist. Yet the fact that these trillions of cells, zillions of atoms, an uncountable numbers of subatomic particles, are behaving perfectly and consistently, just as they do, is proof positive that this design really does exist. These basic particles do not ever act randomly, inconsistently, or out of control. They obey the laws of nature.

This is what we are. This is why we are. This is what everything is made out of. But as we move though our daily lives, fully dependent on everyone of these levels, which are operating inside of us, we give them no thought at all. Talk about shallow thinking!

In fact, *everybody* goes through life dealing with what we can see, hear, taste, smell, and feel. We give virtually no thought to the physical roots of all these things. Only scientists, real scientists, are out there, looking deeper into things. And they serve humanity greatly when they actually observe something new that no one has ever seen before.

But we always need to be ready to recognize the fake scientists. In the olden days, these people were the "snake oil salesmen" selling their magic elixirs. They are the people who claim they can predict the future and know the unknowable. No one knows how the universe began, if indeed it did. No one knows how life began on earth, or how it will end, if it does.

The obvious fact is that we live on a garden planet. All we need to thrive is within our reach. Someone, who I am completely happy to refer to as God, is holding this all together for us. According to his Gospels, all he asks from us is to love Him and to love each other. That doesn't seem like too much to ask.

I think it is also clear that most of our problems persist because we do not trust each other, yet alone love each other. Selfishness, fear, and anxiety are what fuel our failures to cooperate. If each one of us truly *knew* that the Creator of the universe was aware of us, concerned about us, and was available to help us as we needed, if we'd only ask. Then there would be no place for selfishness, fear, or anxiety; or the problems that flow from them.

I know it can be extremely difficult for a nonbeliever to make the sincere leap of faith necessary to get to the point of complete faith in God. I've made that journey myself. And I know how irrational it seems to be the one selfless person in an apparently selfish world. But it should help you to know there are many millions of people who have already accepted that risk and have survived spectacularly, by the grace of God, including me.

I have survived a lifelong physical disability. I was once paralyzed from the neck down in an auto accident. I have had multiple surgical procedures and injections on my spinal cord. I have suffered every fear, concern, and anxiety that any other person has felt. I have felt the pain of the premature deaths of close family members. I have made as many mistakes as anyone else has. And then I read the Gospels. And that changed everything.

I have seen, and benefitted from, many miracles. There is absolutely nothing, in real science that precludes the existence of God. And because of my own personal experiences, I am now certain God is real. God is aware of us. And God will send us everything we need to thrive in this life, and beyond. And what follows are some of the many example of what I am referring to.

My Miraculous Experiences

That Night in 1971

I clearly recall what happened, but I'm still not certain what did happen.

I was eighteen years old at the time, a freshman in college, and home for the holidays after living five hundred miles from home for the past four months. Of course, I had proven to myself I was a mature, responsible, and independent adult. But being back in my parents' home brought back all the old rules I had lived under as a child.

That was not pleasant.

Just for some context, 1971 was just three years after Martin Luther King and Robert F. Kennedy had been assassinated. And three years after the infamous Democrat's National Convention in Chicago. The Vietnam War was in progress, and the nightly news was filled with images of antiwar protests and street riots. The "generation gap" was in full bloom, as long-haired teens were failing to communicate with their Depression- and WW2-era parents. There were no cell phones, no internet, and not even any cable

TV. The country was a mess. And as an eighteen-year-old, I was trying to figure this all out.

So that fateful evening, I went up to my room, alone on the fourth floor of our home in Pittsburgh, to go to sleep. But I never did fall asleep. Instead I began to think about things—everything. I began to reconcile and integrate everything I thought I knew. It was a painstakingly exacting process. I questioned everything I thought was true. I began to realize the inconsistencies I was carrying around. I ended up rejecting many things I had heard along the way. I also had to conclude that some other things, which I hadn't known before, had to be true.

Every assumption I made had to be critically examined and re-examined to be sure there wasn't some form of psychological incentive for me to believe it. Did that assumption imply something complimentary towards me? Did any rejected ideas imply anything derogatory towards me? This was the most rigorous and thorough analysis I had ever undertaken. It was exhilarating.

By 6:30 a.m. or so, it was completed. That night, I had constructed a philosophy of life that integrated everything I knew, both academically and experientially. And it all fit together like a geodesic dome. Every fact supported every other. Every idea supported every other. It was impossible for one of these ideas to be wrong because if it was, then a whole lot more had to also be wrong. It was that interdependent, that internally consistent.

In these intervening forty-eight years, I have actively been seeking proof that some part of this philosophy was incorrect. I knew that even one error would result in an explosion of new learning, which I would have loved to rebuild a new integrated model. I have yet to find that flaw. But I'm still looking.

At the time, I thought I was talking to myself all that night, asking questions and getting great answers. I thought I had done it all alone. But now I'm not sure. How could an eighteen-year-old single handedly construct such a successful philosophy? Given what I now know about God's actions on my behalf, I am more inclined to think that someone else was guiding me then.

That philosophical framework, which was created that night, has been a stalwart companion throughout my life. It has allowed me to grow and learn in a very efficient and successful way. I've never wasted much time on false or irrelevant information. I value everyone's perspective and input on complex issues, and I always seem to get to the best outcomes—both personally and professionally. I have to believe that those ideas were really a gift from "Someone."

Why I Do Not Worry About Money

After I turned forty in the mid-1990s, I decided I should sit down and read the Bible. I knew that for nearly two thousand years, billions of people have believed that the God that created the universe had sent us his only begotten Son to teach us what we needed to know. How could I not read that? And by that age, I felt I was mature enough to accurately judge the veracity of these teachings.

I started with the gospel of Matthew, which in my Bible was only fifty-three pages long. Even though I have a reading disability, I knew I could handle fifty-five pages.

Well, I only got through about twenty pages that evening, which took me about two hours to read. And I was literally overwhelmed by the wisdom and truth that was washing over me with every sentence. I think of myself as a philosopher by nature, and I have read the work of many famous philosophers: Plato, Descartes, Kant, Ortega y Gasset, and many others. I've also read the Tao Te Ching, the Sayings of Confucius, the Dead Sea Scrolls, and Buddhist teachings. None of those writings could hold a candle to the wisdom of the gospels.

That evening changed my life. The one message I was receiving over and over again was, "Don't worry about yourself, take care of others, and God will take care of you." At that point in my life, money was pretty tight. We had a monthly budget, and we knew exactly what our income and expenses were each month. There was precious little money left over, and what there was seemed to go toward unplanned necessities. I was not a "giver." I didn't have anything extra to give away, I thought. That happened on a Wednesday evening.

The next morning, I drove to work, parked my car in downtown Pittsburgh, and was walking along the usual route to my office. For years, I had been passing a panhandler on the way without giving him anything. But the gospel had changed my thinking. It changed my heart, and I changed my behavior. So I gave him one dollar. He said thank you, and I said you're welcome. And on I went to work. The next day, Friday, I saw him again. I said, "Good morning." He said, "Good morning." I gave him a dollar and he said, "Thank you." I said, "You're welcome" and I went on my way. On Monday morning, it was the same brief conversation as I gave him another dollar.

When I got home from work that Monday, I opened the mail to find that I had been sent a check for $63. I wasn't expecting it, but it was for me. Great! On Tuesday, I again had the same exchange as I gave him another dollar. When I got home, I found another check in the mail for me from my car insurance company for $250. About a year earlier, I was involved in a car accident, and I paid my deductible. Their policy was to forgive the deductible if the accident was not your fault. Apparently, it took them a year to figure out it wasn't my fault, and they returned my money. Just like yesterday's check, this one was also unexpected. I had completely forgotten about that accident. If the check had never come, I wouldn't have missed it. But once I saw it, it definitely belonged to me.

The next day, Wednesday, it was the usual: good morning, good morning, dollar, thank you, you're welcome. When I got home, I opened the mail to find a check for $1,825. This one was from the IRS. I was not expecting a tax return. But they informed me I had miscalculated the value of my personal exemptions the previous year, and due to my error, I had overpaid my taxes. At this point, I was having one of the best weeks of my life.

On Thursday morning, I again saw Frank, the panhandler. We later became friends. When I got home, the mail included another check for me in the amount of $500. That check stopped me in my tracks. I finally figured out what was going on. I stopped, looked up toward heaven, and said, "I get it! I get the message. Thank you."

God was telling me I was now on the right path. The message I received from His gospel was the right message. I didn't need to worry about money or from where it would come. God would take of that. My job was to get it to those who needed it. It's hard for me to write this without getting emotional. To finish this story, another check arrived the next day also. I don't recall the amount or details of that one. It wasn't important. I had already gotten the message.

Since that day, money has never been a problem. I began receiving bonuses, stock options, raises, and promotions. I finally peaked out as the president and CEO of a billion-dollar-plus company, before retiring at age sixty-two. I had made it my mission to be as charitable as my wife would let me. But she doesn't know everything. In fact, the gospel specifically instructs that when you are giving money to charity, you should not let your left hand know what your right hand is doing. I only mention it here to illustrate my point.

I remember telling some of our best friends that it seemed like I could not give money away fast enough because more and more kept flowing in. Also, to this day, we still live in the same small house that we bought when we were twenty-four years old. As my daughter once said, when our cup started running over, we did not go out to get a bigger cup.

The most important lesson I learned from this experience had nothing to do with money. I learned that *God is real.* God is aware of us, and our actions, and our thinking. He knows our hearts. And He is willing to actively intercede on our behalf. What could possibly be more important to know than that?

The Day My Father Died

Something happened to me in 1986, October 16.

My father, who was sixty-three years old at the time, was having a "routine" cardiac bypass surgery that morning. The plan was for him to get into post-op around 10:30 a.m. I was planning on getting to the hospital around ten.

Around nine, my sister called to say that the surgery was over but the doctors were having trouble getting him off of the life-support equipment. I should get over there ASAP. Hurriedly, I hopped into the shower, and while there, my father "came to me." He told me he was "leaving now." I stopped in my tracks and said out loud, "No. Wait. Let me get to the hospital."

I quickly rinsed off, got dressed, and drove about twenty minutes to the hospital. When I arrived, I got up to the waiting room and found my mother, sister, two brothers, and some of my mother's friends there. My sister-in-law told me it did not look good. That he was still on the heart and lung machine, and when they tried to remove him from those, his heart did not restart. Shortly after that, a doctor came out and told us the situation was grave. If we would like to go in and visit my father now, it might be the last time.

So we did that. The family had an opportunity to go in and spend some time with him. He was lying there in bed, looking perfectly normal, he appeared to just be sleeping. But we knew the situation was not good. After about fifteen minutes, they escorted us back to the waiting room, and we sat there and waited. As you can imagine, it was not a happy situation. After a while, I decided I did not want to just sit in there. I couldn't take that waiting. So my brothers and I decided to take a walk. My brother-in-law saw us getting up to leave, and he joined us.

While we were grimly walking around the block, outside the hospital, my father came to me a second time. Again he said, "I'm going to go now." Afterwards, I thought about that fact that his children were all grown, educated, and employed. His wife was secure financially. My father grew up during the Great Depression in America, and I knew that those things had always been his primary concerns. So this time, I said, "Okay."

As soon as I said that, I regretted it. Because I knew he was gone. And it seemed as though I had dispatched him. At the same time, I knew we would all be okay. And it really was okay for him to go now. But, it was tough.

At that point, I collected myself and suggested that we go back inside. Everyone agreed, and we took the shortest route back. As we walked down the hall, my sister-in-law came out of the waiting room and told us he had died. Of course, I already knew that.

During the next few days, I asked each of my siblings if they had had any kind of unusual experience during that day. And besides the obvious, none of them had. I don't know why my father decided to talk to me that day. But I believe that, in doing so, he gave me a tremendous gift.

One of the great mysteries of life is whether or not there is life after death. Although the science of near-death experiences has developed significantly in the last thirty-two years, there really is no way to know for a scientific fact, what lies beyond the death of our bodies. This still remains a question of faith.

But in my case, I learned some important facts that day. I learned that my father was going somewhere. His soul, or spirit, or consciousness, or whatever you want to call it, was not contained by his body. And it was going somewhere. So I, for one, know for a fact that our life is more than just our current mortal condition. There is definitely another part of our existence that continues on after our bodily death. And knowing that, has opened up my mind to a much greater sense of what else can be real. My "reality" goes beyond this physical universe. And it includes I don't know what. But I expect to find out, someday. And I expect that I will get a chance to ask my father why he chose to speak to me on his last day on earth.

My Recurring Childhood Dream

I grew up in Pittsburgh, Pennsylvania. And if you know anything about Pittsburgh, you know that there are lots of hills and precious few level streets. As a ten-, eleven- and twelve-year-old child, I rode my bicycle just about everywhere, either up the hills or down the hills. During that period of my life, I used to have this one recurring dream. I would estimate that I had that same dream about four or five times a month.

In the dream, I am riding my bicycle down a steep hill, and at the bottom of the hill the street is flat for just a few yards before it starts up a very long slope. In the dream, I had never succeeded in peddling my bicycle all the way up that slope before. But I was determined to do it this time. As I started up the hill I still had a lot of momentum, and the peddling was easy. About one-third of the way up, I had to start working. I had to make an effort to keep this bike moving. And I was doing pretty well. About two-thirds of the way up, it became a real effort to keep peddling. As I approached about 80 percent of the way up, I began to realize I wasn't going to make it. I thought I would have to get off my bicycle and walk it up the rest of the hill.

Just then, in the dream, I looked down, and I noticed that my bicycle was not a bicycle at all. In fact it was a moped! All I had to do was turn the key on the motor and the engine would come on and power me the rest of the way up the hill. What a great ending to that dream! I made it up the hill, and I did not have to push the bicycle. That was my goal, and I had succeeded.

I didn't know it at the time, but that dream has become the story of my life. When I set an aggressive goal, I do the best I can to get there. But I can never do it alone. Somewhere, somehow, I've always gotten the help I needed to be successful. Honestly, you don't come from immigrant grandparents, as I did, and rise to be the CEO of a successful company on your own. It takes a whole lot of help along the way—great people who have faith in you and who are willing to work to be a part of that success. And again, I have to believe there was a tremendous spiritual component to that help as well. I firmly believe that without God's help, it would not have played out as well as it did.

How I Met My Wife, and Learned About It Thirty Years Later

I was seventeen years old when I left home to attend college near Chicago. I was a math major, and my first college class was in calculus, 9:00 a.m. on a Tuesday morning. My future wife, also a math major, was attending a sister college about six miles away, and that same class was her first class too.

Being the way she is, Mary arrived at the classroom about a half-hour early. The room was empty, so she could pick any seat she wanted. Naturally, she choose the seat in the front row, closest to the teacher's desk. My dorm room was only about one hundred-yards from that classroom, so I naturally arrived about three minutes late. Unfortunately, there was only one empty seat left—in the front row, next to her. Before that class was over, I had borrowed a pencil and some paper from her two hundred-page loose-leaf binder from her. That's how we met. As I said before, I've always seemed to get the help I needed. Four years later, we were married. And have been married now for over forty-three-years. All is well.

Now let's fast-forward thirty years to my high school's thirty-year class reunion, back in Pittsburgh. A friend of mine and I decided to leave the gathering and just walk through the halls of our school. Neither of us had been there in thirty years. As we were walking down the third floor hall, past the administrative offices, toward the steps, I had a "flashback" to an event that happened thirty years earlier, when I was in that exact same spot doing the exact same thing.

As a high school senior, I was a very good student. In fact, out of a class of 304 students from the most academically rigorous school in Pittsburgh, I received the award as the best math student during our graduation ceremony. I had routinely scored in the ninety-eighth percentile on standardized tests. And on math sections, I was always in the ninety-ninth percentile.

Despite all that, as of March during my senior year, I was not planning on going to college. My family had literally no money to contribute to any schooling expenses. It was sad, but hey, that's life.

As "luck" would have it, on this particular date in March of 1971, the same order of Christian brothers who operated my high school also operated a small college outside of Chicago. Furthermore, they were diversifying their student body, and they sent out a gentleman named Brother James Cantwell to recruit students from the more eastern parts of the United States. I had absolutely no interest in talking to this guy. Why would I? I wasn't going to college.

In my flashback, I was walking down this same empty hallway, turning to go down those same steps. Thirty years ago, the hallway was empty because everyone else, except me, was in a class. I have no recollection about how that came be. But there I was. Just as I turned right to head toward the steps, I noticed out of the corner of my eye that the assistant principal, Mr. Mauer, had just stepped out of his office, and there I was. Busted.

In order to avoid the inevitable penalty, for not being wherever I was supposed to be, I smoothly, and imperceptibly altered my path, from the steps, over toward this table full of brochures about this Catholic college. The table was unmanned, which was fine, because I had no interest in the school. I was really just watching to see what Mr. Mauer was going to do.

In a minute or so, Brother Cantwell walked up and engaged me in a conversation. Mr. Mauer was now gone, and I wanted to go too. A few questions into our discussion, Brother Cantwell asked me what my SAT scores were. When I told him, this complete stranger told me that, "if that was true," then he could offer me a full four-year academic scholarship to their college.

Obviously, I had told him the truth, and to make a long story short, I went to college there, majored in math, met my wife in my first class, and went on to get an MBA and have a successful marriage and a successful career. I had totally forgotten how that had happened until thirty-years after the fact. My entire life changed in those few seconds. My children would never have been born. Everything changed.

When I think back on all this, I realize that if Mr. Mauer had come out of his office just three seconds later, or not at all, I would have been safely down the steps and out of sight, having never stopped at that table. Had he been there three seconds earlier, I would have walked right into him and never would have met Brother Cantwell. And why was I even there? I never did things that warranted a punishment. Or if I did, I didn't do them right in front of the administrative offices. I was smart, remember?

I'm sure some people would say this was just a lucky coincidence. But I have experienced so many "lucky coincidences" in my life that I no longer believe in them. Once again, I received exactly what I needed, when I needed it. It is very easy to believe in divine intervention when you have experienced it as often as I have.

I Should Have Died in 1997

In case you are getting the idea that my life has been one pleasant experience after another, I should tell you that in 1976, I came down with something known as Crohn's disease. If you know anyone with Crohn's, then you know how debilitating it is. According to the Americans with Disabilities Act, I have been a disabled person since 1976. But I try not to let it show.

Crohn's is an autoimmune disorder, which causes an inflammation in the intestinal tract. It is incredibly painful. In my case, it also causes potentially fatal internal bleeding. For some time, I was taking 168 prescription drug tablets per week, including some powerful steroids, to treat my symptoms. To this day, I am taking a chemotherapy prescription each day, to keep things under control. This disease seems to have a genetic cause, which makes sense in my case because I had a brother who died at the age of fifteen due to another autoimmune disorder.

My particular type of Crohn's is referred to as "fistulizing Crohn's," which means that my intestinal tract can balloon out in places and begin to grow a new section of intestine. These fistulas are potentially fatal as they can literally grow anywhere, including into a vital organ. They go where they want to go. In my case, a fistula grew out of my small intestine and punched a hole into my large intestine. Strangely enough, that fistula actually saved my life.

Prior to my surgery in 1997, I had developed a 100 percent blockage in my intestinal tract, "downstream" from this fistula. So whenever I ate, the food would move along until it got to the blockage, where it backed up and made my life extremely painful. When it backed up to where the fistula was, the food escaped through the fistula and into my large intestine, which caused me to need a restroom ASAP. I still don't know why that material never leaked out of the hole in my large intestine, which would have caused other serious problems.

Because the food was bypassing dozens of feet of absorption, I was always hungry, which meant more eating, more pain, more internal bleeding, and more problems. Most people I think with 100 percent intestinal blockage, a fully formed fistula, and a hole in their large intestine would probably be dead today.

All these issues came to light when I was hospitalized in 1997 for gastrointestinal bleeding. I literally could not stand up without losing consciousness. When I got to the emergency room, my hemoglobin count was down to 5.0. It took six units of blood to stabilize me. The search for the cause of the bleeding led to the discovery of the fistula. And surgery was scheduled for shortly thereafter.

My internal bleeding, the hole in my intestine, the total blockage, and the fistula were each potential causes for death. But here I am, going strong over twenty years later. To the skeptic, I was just really "lucky" again. But as I continued to benefit from extraordinarily good "luck," my faith in God's intercessions grew ever stronger.

RICHARD KRAULAND

I See Miracles All the Time

At this point in my life, I have been blessed and pro-
tected, by God, so many times that I won't even try to
relate them all. But I will relate two more events to help
you understand how pervasive God's love and help really is.

The first occurred during a 190-mile white-water-raft-
ing trip I took down the Colorado River, through the
entire Grand Canyon. About the third evening, we set up
camp near the confluence with the Little Colorado River.
To make a long story short, I found myself riding down the
rapids in the Little Colorado. Suddenly, I hit my head on
a rock, lost control of myself, and was being washed down
the river. Oh yeah, I forgot to mention I have never learned
how to swim.

So I'm being carried down the river, out of control, and
heading right for a large boulder in the middle of the river.
I was already coughing up water, my head hurt, and I was
trying to breathe in and cough out at the same time. I was
actually happy to see that rock up ahead because I thought
I could grab onto it and regain control of the situation.

Well, that didn't happen. Before I could reach the
rock, the river water was bouncing off it, and the water
pushed me away from, and around, the rock. I was still out
of control. However, as I was moving around the rock, I
was able to make eye contact with a guy who was standing
on the rock. I shouted to him that I needed help. And as
the water was turning me away from him, I heard a splash

in the water behind me. I knew he had dived into the river and was coming to help, even though I couldn't see him.

When he reached me, he lifted my head out of the water, and in a very calm voice, he told me exactly what we were going to do to get out of this river. Within a minute, we were out of the flow, and I was sitting on the riverbank. I did not have the strength to stand up yet. But I thanked him, told him I was okay, and I just needed to sit there for a while to regain my strength.

When I could stand up, I looked to find him. He was in our group of twenty-six rafters, but I hadn't spoken to him up to that point. I found him, thanked him again, and stopped to chat with him and his family. It turned out that he was a fire chief in Ocala, Florida, and he had risen through the ranks by starting out as a…wait for it…a water rescue professional. Once again, I found myself in a difficult situation, and God put exactly the person I needed, right in front of me. Just lucky? I don't think so.

Okay, just one more story. I could go on, but I think my point is crystallizing here. One January weekend in the 1990s, my older brother and I were driving down the Pennsylvania Turnpike, heading to Harrisburg. The weather was terrible, and there were about six inches of icy slush on the road surface. I was trying to stay in the tracks, left by someone else, in the slush. I was only going about 40 mph.

Suddenly, a very large tractor-trailer began slowly passing me on my right side. The front of my car began to rotate to the left, pointing toward the median. I started steering to the right and the car stopped rotating left and began rotating to the right, clockwise. I couldn't get it to straighten out, and the car rotated passed straight, and continued moving to the right. The rear axles of the tractor-trailer were just passing my passenger side door when I realized I was going to rotate my front right side into his rear tires.

So I began steering left. Once again, my car stopped rotating right and began heading back to the left, rotating counterclockwise now. The truck slowly passed me, but I was out of control. At this point we kept rotating until we were sliding forward but facing backward. Then we we're facing toward the right berm, after which we finished our 360-degree spin, slid through the berm, down the slope, and came to a rest down by the drainage ditch, completely off the road-level surface.

Just as we stopped, my brother started to ask me if I was okay, but I only heard his first couple words, because just then another tractor-trailer roared by us. It was in the right lane closest to us. If we had still been on the road surface, our vehicle would have been wiped out. But this story isn't over.

I got out to check the vehicle, the turnpike had these yellow reflector post along the edge of the berm, and I was certain we had crashed through a few of them. When I couldn't find any obvious damage on the car, I looked at the trail we had left in the snow. Our trail missed one reflector post by just a few inches, and the next one by about a foot.

Somehow, we had slid between them, out of control, without touching either one. Crazy.

The next thing I knew, within seconds, a big PennDOT plow truck stopped on the berm, two big guys climbed out and offered to help push us back onto the road level. Thanks to their help, we were quickly back up and driving. This entire ordeal lasted only about four or five minutes. Once we were driving again, it was almost hard to believe it had even happened.

While being out of control, we had just missed hitting the wheels of that first truck passing us, just missed hitting the median wall, just missed getting hit by the truck that roared by, and just missed hitting any reflector posts on our way to the ditch. Then, help showed up immediately, and we were on our way with no damage at all. As I always like to tell everyone, if you say your prayers every day, never try to hurt anyone, and always try to help everyone that you can, then you can be "lucky" too!

I have a lot more true stories like these. But I think I've made my point. God is real. He is aware of each of us. And he is ready to intercede on our behalf. Once you realize that there will never be a reason to worry or fear anything again. Two scripture passages come to mind here: "Ask and you shall receive," and, "If God is with you, who can stand against you?"

A lot of people say they are religious. But my test for that is to see how much peace the person exhibits. If you are anxious, sad, fearful, worrisome, or anything like that, then you need to examine the strength of your faith. On the other hand, if you *know* that God is sending you whatever help you need, then you will not fear. The greatest thing about all this is that *it is true*. Please open your mind. It is your decision. You have the free will to decide this for yourself, right now. If you need more encouragement, please read the gospels.

This is on you.

Do it.

God bless you.

Economics

Okay, enough about science and religion. Let's get down to day-to-day business—economics and wealth creation.

I have spent many years in the business world, and I don't think anything is more misunderstood than business. So let's take a shot at understanding this most common of human activities, starting with the basics.

The most natural activity anyone could possibly do is to solve their own problems. If you're hungry, you find something to eat. If you're thirsty, you find something to drink. If it's very cold or raining or snowing, you find shelter. If your shelter has a hole in the roof, you patch it. If you would rather be in a better climate, you go there, if you can afford it.

All these are examples of actions, which solve a problem. I call them "value creation." And the "value" they create are the solutions you wanted.

This concept of "value" is a very subjective and temporary thing. If you haven't eaten anything for a day or two, then a simple sandwich might be of great value to you. You'd need it. You'd want it. Really want it. As opposed to, let's say, an hour after you have just finished a very large

Thanksgiving Day dinner. At that point, you probably couldn't stand to even look at a sandwich. So the value of something can change from place to place, and from time to time.

Another example might be that leak in your roof. If you have one, then you may be in great need of a roofer to fix your roof. And wouldn't it be great if your neighbor just happened to be one. However, if your roof is in fine shape, then you would have no need to call on him professionally. So the very same object, the sandwich, or your neighbor the roofer, can have great value or little value depending on the circumstances.

So who decides what the circumstances are? Who decides what is valuable, and when? The fact is that each of *us* gets to decide that. We are the only ones who know what we need, what we want, and when. We, individually, decide how valuable something is to us right now. Knowing that our priorities can change from moment to moment, depending upon what our problems are. Actually, we are the only ones who can possibly know what we want right now. No one else could possibly know our needs better than ourselves.

This is a simple, but important fact, because the success or failure of entire economic systems depends on that simple fact. That fact is why human freedom must be the key to any economic system that mankind can develop. The logic is clear. The goal of any economic system should be to create the most value as possible. And value is defined as meeting people's needs and desires, that is, solving people's problems. Thus, the most efficient way to solve those problems is to allow the people who have them, to make the decisions about what they need and when. Another way to say this is, decentralized decision-making.

The principal problem with failed economic systems, such as socialism or communism, is that they ignore this simple fact. Those systems believe that someone at the top of the government is better suited to decide how many sandwiches must be made each day—how many roofers need to be trained and where to put them, how many cars should be built, and houses, and airplanes, and grocery stores, and so on. But if I need a car and the government's sends me a roofer, or a sandwich, well, you can see my point. That roofer or sandwich is not meeting my needs, and therefore, they are not creating value. And while they are wasting their time with me, someone else is going hungry or has a leaky roof.

The concept of a "free market" is no more than this. When I'm hungry, I should be free to find a sandwich shop. And if I can't find one, then my neighbors probably can't find one either, so it might be a great time for me to open a sandwich shop that will meet the needs of me and my neighbors. Furthermore, in a perfect world, I shouldn't have to wait months for some government agencies to give me permits and licenses before I can open my shop. All those delays mean that people's needs aren't being met or that they have to drive a few miles away to find their sandwiches. All of which is a waste of their time and transportation costs. In other words, my shop would be more "efficient" for them. That's good for them. Plus, I get to make a "profit" on their sandwiches. That's good for me. By saving them from those inefficiencies, I am earning my profit.

Which brings us to the concept of "profit." This is another widely misunderstood concept. Let's stick with the example of my sandwich shop, and let's pretend we are watching a video of a typical transaction. When a hungry person walks in the door, let's stop the recording. The scene is frozen. What do we see? There's the hungry customer with money. There is me behind the counter with food. That's all that is in the picture. Now, we hit play again, and we see the customer order his sandwich, I prepare it, he pays for it, and begins walking toward the door. Let's stop the video again. What do we see? Just as before, there is me and the customer. There is food and there is money. Notice that, when comparing this freeze frame to the earlier one, there is exactly the same amount of food, money, and people in the picture. Nothing has been added or subtracted. But "value" had been "created"!

This is the miracle that occurs in every "free" human economic transaction. I cannot overstate this point. We have just watched the creation of human value out of thin air. No one was exploited; no one was robbed. Without adding anything to the picture, the customer is happy now because he has exactly the sandwich he wanted to satisfy his hunger. And he bought it at a price he was willing to pay. If not, he wouldn't have bought it. And I am happy because I opened my shop in order to sell sandwiches and make a profit. And I just met my goals. So both parties to this transaction have gained something from it. This is not a zero-sum gain. Both sides have gained. Both are happier. One is less hungry, and the other is more profitable. Life is better for both. This is capitalism in its purist and simplest form.

And let's not overlook the role that my profit played in this case. The profits I make on my sandwich sales are the reason I am willing to keep my shop open. That is my incentive to be there. Furthermore, I will be using all my profits to help me meet my other needs. My profits will be spent on my housing, my roofer or plumber or carpenter (if I need them), my entertainment, my transportation, or whatever I want. And every time I spend my money on any of those things, that other person will make a profit. So again both his and my needs will be met. More value creation!

This same concept can be scaled up to include huge corporations. Let's face it, no single person could completely print this book by themselves. They'd need paper and ink and equipment, which they probably don't know how to make. Likewise with cars, houses, computers, appliances, you name it. In order to make these complex products people organize themselves into corporations. Let's take an energy company for example. In order to deliver electricity to our homes, it takes someone to make the transmission lines, someone to install them, someone to build and operate the power plants, and still others to mine or drill for the natural resources that are consumed in the power plant. And let's not forget the manufacturers of the light bulbs, TVs, computers, and appliances, which make the electricity useful.

Every one of these creations is the result of countless individuals who have trained to perform their small but important part of the value chain. Their efforts are organized by management. And management teams co-operate freely across great distances and diverse industries in order to pull this all together. That is what corporations do. They are the vehicle by which all these inputs are organized and controlled, for the good of all involved. Corporations are good. Corporations are necessary. If we expect to create enough value to feed, clothe, shelter, educate, inform, and entertain billions of people, corporations will be needed to play a major role.

In truth, if you are indoors right now, look around you. Everything you can sense is there because somebody needed it or wanted it, and probably somebody else, usually corporations, made it for them to meet their desire. Everything we have is there because of the incentives that profit created. Profits are good. Profits are necessary. And history is filled with examples of colossal failures when someone has tried to eliminate the profit from economic transactions. These failures are often referred to as recessions, or depressions, or sometimes even societal collapse.

These failures are inevitable whenever anyone, usually governments, place too many restrictions on the opportunities for people to make their own free choices. This is why communism and socialism have always failed, and always will. Even a cursory look at Venezuela in the twenty-first century will clearly illustrate this point. Regardless of the motives of the leaders, anyone who overly restricts human freedom, usually with laws and regulations, is creating disastrous results. By definition, they are reducing the creation of value that would otherwise exist for all to share. Tragedy always follows.

So as economic systems go, capitalism—that is wisely and properly regulated, with minimal intrusions on human freedom—will always be the most successful system to create human value. Its reliance on human freedom is the key. There are dangers, of course. Not all free people behave morally or honestly. That is a part of our nature too. Such people will always be identified through their behaviors, and they will not last long. More on that in a moment.

Other systems that are based on central planning cannot hope to succeed as well or as efficiently. They simply cannot be in close enough touch with the complex needs that they are trying to satisfy, to meet them. Waste, corruption, and inefficiencies abound. History has proven that time and time again.

And one more thing, while we are on the subject of human nature and its effect on our economics, I'd like to address one other major misconception, which I think is out there, even though it is not true. And that is, the general impression that the public has about businesspeople.

Let me ask you, what comes to mind when you hear the terms *corporation, salesman,* or *businessman*? If you've been watching movies or television shows for the last sixty years, as I have, then you may have a very negative impression of those people. Corporations are being depicted as evil empires where cutthroat promotion-seekers and merciless greed runs rampant. Successful salesmen are usually presented as either aggressive young people who are working themselves into an early grave, or as liars and cheats who will do or say anything to make a sale. Nothing could be further from the truth.

The best salesperson I ever worked with was an immigrant woman from Slovenia. She was well into her sixties when I met her, and she spoke English with a mild accent. This lady worked for the credit union I was running at the time. She was devoted to explaining, to everyone, the benefits of banking with the credit union instead of with a bank. When she was in the checkout line at the grocery store, she would ask the person behind her if they were a member of our credit union. If they said no, then they were about to get an education in personal finance. Every product or service she ever sold was a benefit to her customer. If she couldn't help someone, then she would just move on to the next prospect. She never lied to, or cheated, anyone. And she was incredibly successful. To this day, I hold her up as the ideal example of an excellent salesperson. She was great.

I myself spent many years in sales at a large regional bank. My success came from my ability to understand my customers' concerns and to find solutions to their problems. To do that well, you have to *really* care about helping people. You can't fake that. People can tell. And of course, actually solving real problems, and thereby creating value for your customers, is how you succeed in sales long term.

When you are really good, you no longer even have to sell because your existing customers will refer you to their friends. It would never occur to me to lie or cheat a customer. The damage to my professional reputation would far outweigh any benefit from the ill-gotten sale. And as a manager, I would never hire a liar or a cheat because they would only damage the reputation of my business.

The same is true for businesspeople in general. Let me ask you, if there were three pizza shops near your home that delivered pizza, one was just not great pizza; the second had great pizza, but typically took ninety minutes to deliver, and the pizza was often cold; while the third delivered great pizza in about thirty minutes, which one would you call? Obviously the third. And that is exactly how successful businesspeople become successful. By satisfying their customers. Creating value. Giving people what they want, what they are willing to pay for. It's very simple actually. And the profit they earn is just their share of the value that they created for their customers. They deserve that profit.

Now let's take this principle up a notch. I have many friends and customers who own or operate medium-sized businesses. As such, they depend on their employees and their suppliers to perform as they are expected to perform. And they expect their customers to pay for services rendered under the agreed-upon terms. What do you think they would do with a supplier who sent them damaged goods, or who failed to meet their delivery promises or other contractual terms? Most likely they would try to work it out, and maybe give them a second chance. But if someone proved to be unreliable, they would have to find another supplier. That's the same thing you would do if you were in their shoes.

Likewise with employees. Nothing is greater to an employer than to have a good employee, as many as possible. And under normal operating conditions, good employees do not get fired. Their boss loves them because the customers love them. If you are looking for job security, then have a positive attitude, show up on time, and do a great job. Really, that's it. That's what makes an employee successful. And successful employees make a business successful. There's nothing underhanded, greedy, or malicious involved.

Now let's look at really large corporations. If there's a structural problem in American business, I think it comes out of very large corporations. As companies succeed, they gain more customers, they provide more products, and they need more employees. That is where success can take you in business, and when it does, a new set of issues arise.

Bureaucracies

One of the worst inventions mankind has ever developed is bureaucracy.

Whenever a very large group of people get together, I mean hundreds—or thousands, or more—in order to accomplish a shared goal, they usually end up forming a bureaucracy. The military, government agencies, and large corporations are perfect examples of bureaucracies.

In most all businesses, for example, there are employees who deal directly with the customers. And they often have first-line supervisors who also often get involved to make the customers happy. Likewise, all businesses have an owner, or a president, who care very much about the success of the business. Those people at the top are responsible for everything that goes on there. In smaller companies that might be all there is. But as a business succeeds, it grows. And that means more customers and more employees. And at some point in its growth, the president will need help to oversee everything that is going on.

Over time and with increasing growth, the first-line supervisors will begin to report to an office manager, who may report to a district manager, who reports to a regional manager, who reports to an executive vice president, who reports to the president.

In the military, you have platoon leaders who report to company commanders that report to battalion chiefs, and so on, all the way up to the president. Every civilian branch of the government has its own hierarchy also, which eventually gets up to a cabinet secretary, and then to the president. All of which probably is very necessary and sensible. They are not the biggest problem.

The problem comes from the tools, which the leader has to guide his organization. It is universally the case that in large organizations the leaders set the policies by which everything is controlled. Those policies are spelled out in great detail through the use of procedure manuals. And those procedure manuals are implemented and enforced by the middle managers who reside between the president and the customer contact staff. And that's where the trouble starts.

In the business world, these organizations were initially successful because they did a great job at meeting their customers' needs. Every customer is different, and over time, even the same customer's needs will change. So the business needs to be flexible enough to adapt to those changing needs. Unfortunately, one thing that doesn't change, and isn't flexible, is a written procedure manual. That, combined with the fact that the president, who now has to oversee thousands of people, rarely has any time to spend with customers.

So then, larger companies get to a point where they are not as good as they used to be. The employees are required to follow the policies and procedures, instead of listening to their customers.

I once worked in such a bureaucracy. And I saw firsthand that employees were rewarded for doing just that. If an employee deviated from the policies for any reason, they had better be 100 percent correct because if anything went wrong, their job was in jeopardy. But if they followed the policy, and everything went wrong, the employee was safe. Those kinds of counterproductive incentives are inevitable in any bureaucratic organization.

I am always amused when I hear about huge financial firms, which have been labeled by the government as "too big to fail." To my way of thinking, a better description of them would be "too big to succeed." These firms have become so large, so diversified, and so bureaucratic that there is no hope for any human being to be able to operate and control them properly. We see this play out time and time again, as once great companies disintegrate. General Electric is one such example, which has been in the news lately. It seems to be a part of the natural life cycle of very large businesses.

Besides the additional challenges that size and complexity introduce to a growing successful company, another pathology eventually presents itself. That is the arrival of middle managers. Very large bureaucracies develop layer after layer of middle management. Many of these people do not come up through the ranks. They may be MBAs, CPAs, lawyers, or other college graduates, who come directly into management positions from outside the company. These individuals may have never met a customer.

I've come to think of some of these people as "denizens of the bureaucracy." They are career-oriented people who succeed by working hard to make their boss, and his or her boss, like them. They tend to become politically astute, and they are driven to be promoted. What they can be completely oblivious to is the customer base. To them customers are numbers on a spreadsheet or a management report. As a class of people, I believe many middle managers are more selfish than the customer-contact staff. And in the long run, the less of these people you have the better. My sense is that government agencies have been virtually overrun by this type of person.

And speaking of the government, they are the grand-daddy of all bureaucracies. I believe that there are now over two million people working for the United State's federal government. Every organizational pathology that exists in human nature is present in the government's bureaucracy. Please understand, I'm not saying that the people who work there are all bad. I'm sure the majority may want to be very good people. But the environment in which they work requires them to do counterproductive and wasteful things, in order to "succeed."

Also, quite honestly, the government does not "have a heart," in the human sense of being caring, thoughtful, or kind. The people there may be very caring. But they don't run the show. It is the policies and procedures that run the show. They are what dictates everyone's actions. The people there show up in their offices for eight hours a day, follow the procedures, and go home. And since they are funded by tax dollars, there is really no organizational incentive to even do a good job. They do not have to create value in order to earn a profit. The intent and outcomes of their actions are not of primary importance, only their adherence to the policies and procedures matter. Under such circumstances, it is virtually impossible to have a responsive and efficient organization.

So this brings us to another uncomfortable fact. When our society, here in the twenty-first century, has a widespread problem like crime, drug addiction, medical care, gun violence, housing, transportation, whatever—people turn to government for solutions. But as we've said, the government is bureaucratic by its very nature. For that reason, it is incapable of providing effective and efficient solutions for anything. When government gets involved, society must still incur the direct cost of fixing the problems. But added to those direct costs are the indirect costs of paying for the bureaucratic overhead, as well as the cost of correcting the inevitable errors that will be caused by the bureaucracy.

The growth of government is one of our major societal ills of the twenty-first century. People who put their hope in government will always be disappointed. The only thing that government can do is to promulgate new laws and new regulations, many of which serve to obstruct right-minded citizens from doing the right things to solve their own local problems. Nevertheless, we continue to send more and more of our hard-earned wealth to the government, where it is squandered on failed attempts at solutions.

In the first year of Donald Trump's presidency, he and the congress eliminated thousands of pages of government regulations. The economy and the stock market reacted by growing at a startling rate. This kind of growth was not thought possible even six months before the election.

Here's an important point: it wasn't President Trump or the congress which created that growth. It was us, the people. Once those regulations were removed, we were freer to take action, solve our own local problems, and thereby, create human value. In economic terms, that value is measured as GDP (gross domestic production). There are still countless thousands of other pages of government regulations. Each one of those is an opportunity, by eliminating it, to free up the people more, to further improve our personal conditions.

Our leaders in government actually have a blind spot when it comes to solving many of society's problems. The correct solutions often involve *less* government, not more. But they can't see that. Their approach it to try to conceive of *more* government actions in order to address the problems. Their actions eventually become laws and regulations, which are enforced by a heartless government bureaucracy.

So what can *we* do? We need to stop seeking solutions from others, from our government. We need to know that just doesn't work. We need to take the approach that it is our responsibility to solve our own problems, and to help those who need help. Let the government do things like national defense and running the court system. And we need to elect leaders who see things this way. I have to believe that if we can eliminate the waste, fraud, and abuse that is inherent in government bureaucracies, then that money could be used to more directly address the problems the money was intended to solve.

Elections matter. And it is our responsibility to support candidates and political parties, which believe in human freedom. And who will maintain a fidelity to our constitution. Politicians who promise you freebies and support expanded government programs are either fools or dishonest. Either way, they don't deserve our support. And any candidate who is promising socialist solutions should be shunned by every voter. That person would be a disaster for any country he or she will ever govern.

And one more point on the subject of voting. It does not matter what sex a candidate is, or what color their skin is, what their sexual orientation is or even what religious tradition they choose to follow. What does matter is their devotion to the concepts of human freedom and human rights, which are enumerated in our constitution and our Declaration of Independence. Human freedom is what drives a successful economy and a strong, diverse, successful country. Anyone who chooses to seek to lead a nation, must, at a minimum, be dedicated to those primary values.

Elections matter. And once again, it is on us, on *you*, to do the right thing. So do it!

Misconceptions and Truths

As a person who seeks the truth, it irritates me to no end that there are so many misconceptions that are floating around in our schools, our media, our science, and our political messaging. Here's is a short list of examples. If you have accepted any of these misconceptions as truth, then I strongly recommend that you identify why you believe them. Who told you that these were true? There may be many sources, as these ideas bounce around and can come at us from all directions.

You should endeavor to stop trusting information from those sources. They may be friends, coworkers, newspapers, websites, news networks, or whatever. Whoever they are, they have been misinforming you. And it is critically important, to your success in life, to be properly and truthfully informed.

Misconception: Socialism is a better economic system than capitalism.

Truth: As we have already explained, socialism has failed everywhere that it has been tried. You can look up the current events in today's Venezuela to see how quickly socialism can destroy a society. Socialism's fatal flaws of centralized decision-making and bureaucratic implementation will always doom it to failure.

Misconception: Capitalism is immoral and exploitative.

Truth: Capitalism, at its core, is based on free human beings freely choosing to engage in economic transactions in which both sides benefit. Thereby, it is the most moral and most productive economic system in human history. Individuals may behave very badly in a capitalistic system, but they will eventually be weeded out. And corporations, which grow beyond their ability to satisfy their customers, will likewise go away.

Misconception: Every country respects human rights.

Truth: The United States virtually invented the institutionalization of a human rights guaranty. No other country has a Bill of Rights in their Constitution. No other country recognizes that our rights come from our Creator. The United States is unique in the world on this score. That trust in free human beings is what makes America great. And that trust is one of the primary reasons why so many people want to come here.

Misconception: We in the United States are in no danger of losing our human rights.

Truth: Every new law and regulation that any state, local, or federal, government passes directly reduces our freedom. We need to reject any candidate or political party that is devoted to solving problems by passing new laws. In truth, eliminating existing laws and regulations will be infinitely more effective in protecting our rights. The only guaranty that we have of maintaining our rights lies in our ability to elect leaders who respect those rights. They can certainly be lost.

Misconception: Most of our society's problems can be solved by more government solutions.

Truth: Government, through its bureaucratic nature, is completely incompetent when it comes to efficiently solving problems. America is great because we have historically allowed our population to freely solve its own problems, while other countries have grown their central government's power. Less government is always better. Less government means more freedom. More freedom means more wealth. More wealth means more opportunities to serve mankind. Please do not put your faith in government solutions.

Misconception: Science knows the universe was created in the big bang, about 15 billion years ago.

Truth: There was no big bang. There were no scientists there to observe it. It is just a theory. And that outdated theory has already been totally discredited by the actual observations of real scientists using superior technology, like the Hubble telescope and others.

Misconception: Evolution can explain the origination of life on earth.

Truth: Evolution may well explain the effect that environment has on a population of existing living organisms, but it has no application to the question of how life *began*. In fact, real scientists now know enough about

genetics, chemistry, and biology, to reasonably conclude that some intelligent designer had to be involved.

Misconception: There is no scientific evidence of God's
existence.

Truth: The very essence of science, the scientific method,
is totally dependent on the principle of universality.
That is the name given to the observable fact that
every atom of every element on the periodic table
(hydrogen, helium, carbon, oxygen, nitrogen, etc.),
behaves exactly the same as every other atom of that
element. Someone has created and is enforcing the
laws of nature, throughout the observable universe.
That Creator is who I refer to as God. The fact that
His nature is infinitely beyond our ability to compre-
hend in no way eliminates the fact that *something* is
actively holding this all together.

Furthermore, recent discoveries in the science of genetics have proven, beyond a reasonable doubt, that some
intelligent designer had to be involved in the origin of life.

And it stands to reason that the same creator was also
this designer.

Misconception: Scientists have firmly proven that manmade global warming will have disastrous effects on
the planet unless we take immediate action to reduce
carbon dioxide emissions.

Truth: All these dire predictions are based on highly complex computer models, which aren't worth the paper

they are printed on. The error factor in these models is compounded by trillions of calculations until it completely overwhelms any calculated predictions. Those predictions are empirically useless. The earth's climate is much more complex than any of our models, and we don't have the necessary data to initiate any model regardless of its complexity.

And on the contrary, real observations of the historical trends in the earth's temperature, support the belief that our environment is being controlled, by Something, in a way that benefits mankind.

Misconception: Every religious faith is equivalent. None is better than the others.

Truth: Many religious faiths share the same values and implications for human behavior. I have found that the Gospels of Christ are readily recognizable as providing us with all the proper instructions we need for living a successful life. But don't take my word for it. Read them! And decide for yourself. In my Bible, the Gospel of Matthew is only fifty-three pages long, Mark is thirty-five, Luke is fifty-five, and John is fifty-four pages. It would be the biggest mistake of your life to ignore the teaching of our Creator God, as delivered to us by his own Son. I beg you to at least read one. And then decide. What have you got to lose?

Misconception: Everybody has a long list of problems to deal with. It might include health problems, financial problems, work problems, relationship problems, whatever.

Truth: In truth, we all have only *one* problem in life. And we all have the same problem. That is, we need to get ourselves right with God, the Creator of the universe and the Intelligent Designer of all life. The Gospels of Christ teach us how to do that. Once we solve our one problem, life still happens—people get sick, accidents happen, financial difficulties can arise, you still might have difficulty getting along with some people, whatever. But when those issues do arise, you will discover that you will have everything you need to deal with them. Calmly. Securely. It's a wondrous thing. You can confidently eliminate worry, fear, and anxiety, from your life. Try it. It works. It is real.

I'm sure there are many more misconceptions that are widely circulating. You can probably think of a few more yourself. But I think I've made my point. For us to achieve a more peaceful and prosperous society, we need to reject all misconceptions and embrace the truths—the truths that are consistent with real scientific facts, logic, and your own daily experiences. Succeeding completely in this endeavor may well be beyond the capabilities of our imperfect selves. But we need to make our best efforts to do so. And then, hopefully, we will get the help we need to fully succeed.

Again, for your own sake, you really need to stop trusting information from those sources, which are disseminating the misconceptions listed above. They may be friends, family, coworkers, newspapers, websites, news networks, or whatever. Whoever they are, they have been misinforming you. Better yet, make an effort yourself to try and inform them of the truth. It is critically important, to your and their success in life, to be properly and truthfully informed. May God bless your efforts. Start today.

So Then,
How Should We Live?

We hold these truths to be self-evident:
That all men are created equal; and they
are endowed by their Creator with certain
unalienable rights, and among these are
life, liberty, and the pursuit of happiness.

—The Declaration of Independence,
AD 1776

I believe that way too many Americans take the idea of human rights for granted. They assume that everyone knows about these rights, that everyone in the world believes in them, and that they could never go away. All three of those assumptions are patently untrue. In 1776, the dominant theories of governance were based on "the divine right of kings," or the most basic "might makes right." And the "might makes right" theory still holds sway across most of the globe.

This idea that humans were made to be free, born with equal dignity, and with a right to work to meet their own needs and wants is purely an American concept when applied to governance. It may be the most important reason to love our country. And we need to be concerned about losing these rights, which are our identity alone. The concept that people are free and that the right to govern comes solely from the consent of the governed is not universally accepted. So we need to be vigilant.

The greatest threat to our human rights is the growth of centralized power—that is, our own government. It is very easy for Americans to understand how *government* is the opposite of *freedom* in countries like North Korea, Russia, China, Cuba, Venezuela, Syria, and many others. But we seem to have a blind spot when applying that same principle here in our own country.

If you believe, as I do, that Jesus was, in fact, the son of God. And that he was sent to teach us what our Creator decided we needed to know. Then you realize that He could have given us any message He wanted to. And here we are, two thousand years later, still talking about what he chose to teach us.

Jesus *could have* traveled to Rome, established a welfare state, raised taxes, and taught us how to run an efficient and compassionate bureaucracy. Feeding and caring for everyone. But He didn't do that.

Instead, He taught us that each one of us needs to treat others in accordance with the golden rule—that we should love God, and love all others as we love ourselves. Our love of God should be manifested in our charitable acts toward other people. This is *our* responsibility, individually, not collectively.

So let's not pretend that Jesus was silent on these points. This is not a matter for idle speculation. His teachings are clear and unmistakable. Socialism and communism are *not* expressions of Christian love. In fact, the power that those kinds of central government systems employ directly conflicts with, and suppresses, the human freedom that God has given to each of us.

In America today, there are active efforts currently underway to make this worse. One of the most insidious efforts is voter fraud. How can we know who the governed are freely consenting to lead them, if the voting results have been corrupted? If an investigation discovers that there are no irregularities that would be wonderful. If it uncovers problems, those problems can be solved. Only those who are corrupting the vote could possibly lose anything in such an investigation. We should actively resist any political party, or candidate, who opposes an open and honest investigation into voting practices anywhere in our country.

The most widespread fuel for larger government comes from the creeping litany of "free stuff" that the government distributes. This is dishonest because nothing is free. Somebody had to work to create any benefit that the government is giving away. And someone else had to pay for it. If you think that you are winning by collecting "free" benefits that you could otherwise earn for yourself, then you have been terribly misled. Search your heart. Where is your happiness? Where is your self-respect and dignity? What is your purpose for living? Is it really worth giving up your freedom for a few dollars per month? And how much more could you earn, and have, if you really made an effort?

Don't send me your answers to these questions. Send them to yourself. Think about them, and believe me, your free benefits are costing you a lot more than you realize. Any candidate or political party that is promoting socialism must be resisted and defeated—both to protect the human rights that we have been given by our Creator and to prevent a failed economic system from causing our country to fail as well.

By the way, I am not referring to benefits for people who have worked all their lives to contribute to our country. Or for those who are disabled, or for any reason unable to support themselves. A free country, with a free capitalist economy can easily generate enough wealth to support those truly needy amongst us. But no economy can support a large population of people who refuse to support themselves, even though they could.

Which brings us to your economic well-being. The secret to being more successful economically is to find a way to serve more people, to make yourself more valuable to your fellow man. By engaging in economic transactions freely, you will create value for yourself, as well as others. Do this as much as you can. It may involve doing more work, being a better employee, spending more time everyday helping others in any way you can, or enhancing your education so you can perform higher-valued activities.

This shouldn't be hard. You should be doing things you are either good at, or things you enjoy doing. Discover what those things are. Do those things in the service of others. Worry less about pleasing yourself and more about serving others. You'll be very surprised how well that will work out for you.

In my own case, I got my first job as a volunteer. I learned fast and did as much work as I could to lessen the load on others. By the time I asked to get paid, it was clear to everyone I was worth it. No one can do that for you.

Contrast that to a friend of mine who once told me his career goal was to make as much money as possible while doing as little work as possible. As you might imagine, he has had great difficulty holding down a job, despite a great education. Your success depends on how much you do for others. And it's up to you to get yourself going.

Unfortunately, getting going may not be as easy as it should be. Because of the growth of our state, local, and federal government, you may well run into a wall of red tape, in the form of zoning, licensing, tax, certifications, permits, and other requirements. They make it a lot harder, but not impossible, to be successful. Don't ever give up. And always vote for the candidate, or political party, which is committed to less government regulations and more personal freedoms. That really makes a difference.

Of course, the most important element in a successful life has to do with developing a belief system, which is based on truth and which helps you to freely find and fulfill your purpose in life. This is again on you. You are responsible for figuring this out. And your success in life is directly proportional to how well you get this right.

Remember, that Someone is holding the entire universe together. Every single molecule, every single atom, every single subatomic particle in the known universe is continuously behaving in a perfectly consistent way. They are not acting randomly, or decaying into oblivion. They consistently and perfectly follow the laws of nature. The power to set and enforce the laws of nature is far beyond our ability to alter or understand. But that is a power we should definitely recognize and respect.

Likewise, remember what we know about the nature of life. A typical human being has over 37,000,000,000,000 cells in its body. And each cell contains about 100 trillion atoms. So for a human being to evolve randomly and accidentally would be the same as if a jigsaw puzzle with over 3,700,000,000,000,000,000,000,000,000 pieces, just randomly came together, all by itself. Also, while that was happening, another human, of the opposite sex, had to be coming together too. And a whole lot of plants and other animals, with trillions of cells of their own, also had to randomly come together at the scene. That is obviously a ridiculous assumption.

Isn't it much more likely that some superior intelligence designed the puzzle and put it together Himself? We already know, from scientific observations, that all these puzzle pieces (atoms) are already being controlled and held together by some controlling force. What other being could there be to make that happen than the Creator? I think all this just stands to reason. To disagree with any of this is to deny scientific observations and to choose to believe in an astronomically impossible event.

I believe in science, real science. I believe in logic. And I believe in God, our Creator. I hope this reading has helped to move you in His direction. For additional help, *please* read the Gospels. They can make you a better person. And you can make the world a better place.

Thank you.

Happy is the man who findeth Wisdom,
and the man who getteth Understanding.

—Proverbs 3:13

And he shall know the Truth. And
the Truth will set you free.

—John 8:32

Why can't we all just get along?

—Rodney King

About the Author

The author's grandparents were immigrant farmers to America circa AD 1900. His parents grew up during the Depression and World War Two, which prevented them from completing even a high school education.

He has been married for forty-four years to his wife who he met in a calculus class. They have two children, both of whom are scientist engineers. His close family circle now includes an electrical engineer, a PhD experimental plasma physicist, a rocket scientist, a PhD biotechnology engineer, and multiple medical doctors and attorneys.

The author describes himself as a philosopher by nature, a mathematician by education, and a builder of a billion-dollar-plus company by profession.

Despite suffering from two lifelong illnesses, and once being temporarily paralyzed from the neck down in an automobile accident, he has experienced remarkable success in life. He says his success accelerated tremendously when he was in his early forties, once he understood what was really going on in the world.

This book is his effort to help everyone to separate the truth from the misconceptions that cause people to fall short of their goals. By applying his new insights, provided by the past fifty years of mankind's incredible scientific advances, he is confident that everyone can be successful in life.

Now in his mid-sixties, Rich is beginning his career as an author, in order to help and encourage others to find their path to happiness and success. It's never too late! Let's get going.

9 781645 696308